A Kid's Cat Library™

Shorthaired Cats in America

Jennifer Quasha

The Rosen Publishing Group's
PowerKids Press™
New York

For Katiana and Mimi

Published in 2000 by The Rosen Publishing Group, Inc.
29 East 21st Street, New York, NY 10010

First Edition

Book Design: Michael de Guzman

Photo Credits: p. 1 © Manuel Denner/International Stock; p. 4 © Richard Shiell/Animals Animals; p. 7 © Orion/International Stock and CORBIS-Bettmann; p. 8 © Gerald Lacz/Animals Animals; p. 11 © The Bridgeman Art Library International Ltd; p. 12 CORBIS/Hulton-Deutsch Collection; p. 15 CORBIS/Michael T. Sedam; p. 16 The Everett Collection; p. 19 © Margot Conte/Animals Animals; p. 20 © Renee Stockdale/Animals Animals.

Quasha, Jennifer
    Shorthaired cats in America / by Jennifer Quasha.
        p.   cm. — (A kid's cat library)
    Includes index.
    Summary: Discusses the history of non-pedigreed shorthaired cats in America.
    ISBN 0-8239-5513-3
    1. American shorthair cat—Juvenile literature. [1. American shorthair cat. 2. Cats.] I. Title. II. Series: Quasha, Jennifer. Kid's cat library.
    SF449.A45Q36   1999
    636.8'22—DC21   98-53561
                                                      CIP
                                                       AC

Manufactured in the United States of America

Contents

Shorthaired cats are great pets. Their short fur makes them easy to care for.

▼

Shorthaired Cats

The United States has more cats than any other country in the world. There are 64 million cats living in American homes today. While some of these cats have long hair, most are shorthaired cats. This is because the **ancestor** of today's housecats, the North African wildcat, was a shorthaired cat. Some housecats may be of a certain **breed**, like Siamese or Persians. Most though, are not a special breed. They're just everyday shorthaired cats, each special in its own way.

Shorthaired Cats at Sea

The shorthaired cat came to America at the same time as the Pilgrims. At that time, cats were kept on ships to **protect** sailors' food from rats that had gotten aboard. There was at least one cat on the famous Mayflower ship when it landed in America in 1620.

Once in America, the settlers were glad to have cats to help them. In the early 1700s, Pennsylvania **colonists** had large numbers of cats sent from England to hunt **rodents** in their barns and homes.

Rats and mice aboard the Mayflower could have eaten food supplies and might have even spread diseases. The cat on board helped keep the ▶ rodent population down and the passengers safe.

Cats and Witches

Many American colonists thought that cats were evil. This was because beginning in the 1400s, religious leaders in Europe said that people who **worshipped** cats were witches and should be burned. When the English came to America, they brought this belief with them.

In 1692, in a Massachusetts town called Salem, people began **accusing** others of being witches. The **evidence** against one woman, Sarah Good, was that she had been seen with a cat. Later people realized that there were no witches and that cats were not evil. Unfortunately, 20 villagers had been hanged before people realized their mistake.

◄ *People in the colonies thought that black cats were especially evil. Today, some people still believe that black cats bring bad luck.*

Shorthaired Cats in Art

By the 1800s, Americans no longer felt that cats were witches' **companions**. Cats had become important members of the family. At that time, the camera was just being invented. When a person wanted a picture of himself or a family member, he had to pay someone to paint it. Cats were such an important part of people's lives that they wanted their cats to be in the paintings, too. American artists like George White, John Bradley, and Ammi Phillips often painted pictures of people at home with their shorthaired cats.

John Bradley painted this picture of a girl and her shorthaired kitten around 1840. ▶

American Cats at War

World War II was fought in Europe in the early 1940s. After the war, people did not have a lot of food to eat. The U.S. government sent food shipments to the country of France to make sure that people there would not go hungry. Since the French had less food than usual, the food they did have needed to be protected from rodents. In 1948, thousands of stray American cats were rounded up and sent to France to guard the food. This brave effort was called the "Cats for Europe Campaign."

Shorthaired cats helped people in World War II by keeping their food safe from rodents and by being good companions.

A Working Cat

The only work most cats normally do is hunt rats and mice. A cat in Columbia, Washington, had a more unusual job. A 500-foot pipe in the Grand Coulee Dam was becoming clogged. Workers didn't know how they would clear such a long pipe. Then they got the idea to use one of the cats that lived in the area of the dam. They tied a string to the cat and sent the cat walking through the pipe. The workers had a machine to blow air into the pipe to help the cat through. The cat unclogged the pipe and kept the dam working smoothly.

A shorthaired cat helped to fix this huge dam in Washington. The dam controls how much water flows into parts of the river.

Tom and Jerry

Cats in Cartoons

Shorthaired cats have been the stars of many American cartoons. In 1913, the artist George Herriman first drew a cartoon called "Krazy Kat." "Krazy Kat" was about a cat that was in love with a mouse. The mouse didn't like Krazy Kat and threw bricks at him. People loved Krazy Kat, though. They loved him so much that other cartoonists began to draw cats, too. In 1919, Otto Messmer created Felix the Cat in a movie called *Feline Follies*. Later, even more cartoons were created about cats. "Tom and Jerry" and "Garfield" were both popular cartoons about shorthaired cats.

Krazy Kat ▶

◀ *Garfield*

Morris the Cat

One of the most famous shorthaired cats in America is Morris. He is known by millions of Americans for his cat food commercials on television. Morris's real name was Lucky. He was discovered at an animal shelter in Illinois by a man named Bob Martwick. Morris first appeared on television in the early 1970s. Since then, he has earned millions of dollars and is recognized by people all over the country. In 1973, Morris won an award called the Patsy award. The Patsy award is given to an animal who has starred on television or in the movies. Morris really was a lucky cat!

Morris was found in an animal shelter like this one.
Animal shelters help find homes for stray animals. ▶

Cats Helping People

Many doctors and scientists believe that being around cats can make people healthy. Studies have shown that people who own cats die less often from heart problems than people who do not own cats. This is because petting a cat can help lower high **blood pressure**, which is bad for a person's heart. Some doctors believe that owning a cat can make people happier and more relaxed. They use **pet therapy** to help patients who are having **emotional** problems. Taking care of a cat makes people feel **responsible**. Owning a cat also helps people love and feel loved.

◀ *Petting a cat can help you feel better when you're upset.*

Shorthaired Cats in America Today

Shorthaired cats have been useful to Americans throughout history. They have posed for paintings and made us laugh in cartoons. They have helped hunt rodents and kept people healthy. Their most important place, though, is in people's families. People like having cats as pets because they are beautiful and loving animals. Shorthaired cats are important in both America's history and in our homes today.

Web Sites:

http://www.lam.mus.ca.us/cats/
http://www.best.com/~sirlou/cat.shtml

Glossary

accuse (uh-KYOOZ) To say that someone is bad or that he or she did something bad.

ancestor (AN-ses-tur) A relative who lived long ago.

blood pressure (BLUD PREH-shur) The pressure created in your veins when your heart pumps blood through your body.

breed (BREED) A group of animals that look very much alike and have the same kind of relatives.

colonist (KAH-luh-nist) A person who lives in a colony.

companion (kum-PAN-yun) A person or animal that goes with someone else and shares in what he or she is doing.

emotional (ih-MOH-shuh-nul) Having to do with strong feelings, such as anger or sadness.

evidence (EH-vih-dints) Facts that prove something.

pet therapy (PEHT THER-uh-pee) When people use animals to help them deal with physical or emotional problems.

protect (PRUH-tekt) To keep from harm.

responsible (rih-SPON-sih-bul) Being the one to take care of someone or something.

rodent (ROH-dint) A kind of animal, such as a mouse, rat, or squirrel.

worship (WUR-ship) To pay great honor and respect to someone or something.

Index